# STRANGE
# BUT TRUE
# CATS

SWEETWATER
PRESS

*Strange But True Cats*

Copyright © 2006 by Cliff Road Books, Inc.
Produced by arrangement with Sweetwater Press

All rights reserved. No part of this book may be
reproduced in any form or by any electronic or
mechanical means, including information storage and
retrieval systems, without written permission from the
publisher.

ISBN-13: 978-1-58173-619-9
ISBN-10: 1-58173-619-3

Cover design by McGinty
Book design by Pat Covert

Printed in China

# STRANGE BUT TRUE CATS

SWEETWATER
PRESS

# CONTENTS

# RECORD SETTERS: CATS THAT CAN'T BE BEAT

The Ragdoll and the Maine Coon are the biggest cat breeds, weighing 20 pounds or more.

The Singapura is the smallest breed of cat.

The most recently documented smallest cat is Mr. Peebles, a domestic short hair that resides in Pekin, Illinois. He is only 6.1 inches tall, 19.2 inches long, and weighs 3 pounds.

The world's fattest cat was a neutered male tabby named Himmey, owned by Thomas Vyse of Queensland, Australia. When Himmey died of respiratory failure, he weighed a whopping 46 pounds.

I really need to lay off the doughnuts.

The first cat show took place in 1871 at the Crystal Palace in London. The first North American cat show was held in New England in the 1870s.

A tabby named Dusty gave birth to 420 kittens in her lifetime.

The largest kitten litter on record was produced by a Burmese/Siamese cat in 1970. There were 19 kittens; however, 4 of them were stillborn.

Another impressive litter was born to a Persian named Bluebell, who gave birth to 14 kittens, all of which survived.

Kitty, owned by George Johnstone of Staffordshire, UK, gave birth to 2 kittens at age 30. During her life, Kitty produced a total of 218 kittens.

Towser, a rodent control tortoise-shell tabby in Scotland, killed 28,899 mice in her 21 years.

The oldest living cat is Creme Puff of Austin, Texas. Born on August 3, 1967, Creme Puff celebrated her 38th birthday in August 2005.

This is the last time I pose for that idiot's Christmas card.

Can I help you with something?

Another old cat is a Burmese
called Kataleena Lady who lives in
Melbourne, Australia. She was born on
March 11, 1977.

Other cats of notable ages:

• Puss, who was born in 1903 and passed away in 1939, one day after his 36th birthday.

• Ma, owned by Alice St. George Moore of Drewsteignton, England. Ma was put to sleep in 1957, at the age of 34 years.

• Grandpa, who was adopted from the Humane Society in Texas, lived to be 34.

American Shorthairs were the first pedigreed breed recognized in the United States.

A 5-year-old moggy named Jake has 27 toes.

Another cat, Mooch, is recorded as having 28 toes.

A cat named Hamlet escaped from his carrier while on a flight from Toronto. He was discovered 7 weeks later behind a panel. It is estimated that he traveled 600,000 km.

An Asian Leopard Cat/Domestic Shorthair hybrid, bred by Esmond Gay, is the world's most expensive cat. Zeus has an asking price of £100,000!

Louis, I think this is the beginning of a beautiful friendship.

Andy, who was owned by a Florida senator, holds the world record for the longest non-fatal fall. He fell from the 16th floor of an apartment building.

A cat remained alive in a collapsed building 80 days after an earthquake in Taiwan in December 1999.

Ben Rea left his cat Blackie, now the world's richest cat, £15 million in his will.

Oh, no, you didn't!

Jack & Donna Wright of Kingston,
Ontario, hold the world record for most
cats owned: 689.

Step away from the box. I repeat: step
away from the box.

Verismo Leonetti Reserve Red is 48 inches tall from the tip of his nose to the end of his tail.

Phoenician cargo ships are thought to have brought the first domesticated cats to Europe around 900 BC.

The first breeding pair of Siamese cats arrived in England in 1884.

The Proailurus, the first true cats, came into existence about 12 million years ago.

Wastin' away again in Margaritaville.

# CAT-ATOMICALLY CORRECT

Although kittens are blind at birth, the touch receptors in their noses are already developed. Thus, rubbing noses with their mother is what helps kittens make contact and feel secure.

Light is reflected from a layer of mirror-like cells called the tapetum lucidum, found just behind the retina. These cells help cats see in very low light by reflecting all available light back into the retina.

More than 20 muscles in each ear enable cats to rotate their ears in many directions, allowing them to pinpoint the source of a sound easily.

When it comes to low-pitched sounds, cats have a similar range of hearing as humans. But cats have a much greater ability to hear very high-pitched sounds; their keenness is even better than that of dogs.

Cats can judge within 3 inches
the precise location of a sound being
made one yard away—an essential
predatory skill.

Hey, ever heard of knocking?

A cat can rotate its ears independently 180 degrees, and can turn in the direction of sound 10 times faster than a watchdog.

This is nothing. You should see what happens during a full moon.

Humans generally start to feel uncomfortable when their skin temperature rises to about 112 degrees, but cats don't start to feel uncomfortable until their skin temperature reaches about 126 degrees.

The gene that results in the orange, tortoise-shell coat pattern of a calico cat is linked to the gene that determines a cat's sex. A cat with this coat pattern is usually female, but on the rare occasion it is a male, he's usually sterile.

Cats walk on their toes, allowing them to prowl noiselessly.

Cats step with both left legs, then both right legs when they walk or run.

The cat's lack of a shoulder blade allows freedom of movement of the foreleg, which can be turned in almost any direction.

Cats can compress or elongate their spine, enabling them to sleep in tight places or leap across large spaces.

Wasted again.

A cat may twitch his whiskers, flex his paws, or move his tail while in a deep sleep. Some scientists also think cats dream.

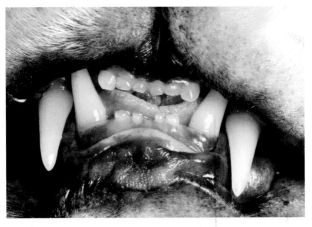

My uncle on my mother's side was a vampire bat.

Cat's aren't color blind—they can see green, blue, and red.

A cat's teeth are very sharp, and finely serrated like a knife. The curved, pointed canines are set in the cat's jaw so that the molars fit together with their sides intact, like a pair of scissors, rather than tooth to tooth.

The average cat's heart beats about 110 to 140 times a minute—that's twice as fast as human hearts.

Cats can have acne.

The top two rows of a cat's whiskers can move independently of the lower two rows, allowing maximum perception of its immediate surroundings.

Cats have 30 vertebrae and lack a collarbone.

A cat's field of vision is about 185 degrees.

You, in the back of the room. Care to
share with the rest of the class?

Most cats do not have eyelashes.

Cats have 32 muscles that control the
outer ear.

Cats with white coats and blue eyes are commonly deaf.

The whiskers of a cat are capable of registering very small changes in air pressure.

Cats have 5 toes on each of their front paws and 4 toes on each back paw.

Some are polydactyl, or many-toed, and
can be born with as many as 7 front
toes and extra back ones.

But how does it work exactly?

If you'd get that camera out of my face,
I wouldn't be so frightened.

A cat's hair stands up evenly all over the body when frightened, but only in a

narrow band along the spine and tail when threatened or ready to attack.

Cats have a sense of smell that is fourteen times stronger than a human's.
Cats have 100 different vocalization sounds.
In relation to body size, cats have the largest eyes of any mammal.

It takes as long as 2 weeks for kittens to hear well. Their eyes usually open between 7 and 10 days, but can open in as little as 2 days.

A cat sees about 6 times better than a human at night.

A cat's hearing is 5 times greater than that of a human.

The Jacobson's organ is located in the roof of a cat's mouth and analyzes smells.

My contacts have been in way too long.

Cats take 20 to 40 breaths per minute.

Declawing a cat is equivalent to cutting a human's finger off at the first knuckle.

Oops, you caught me.

A female cat can begin mating when she is between 5 and 9 months old and will be pregnant for approximately 9 weeks.

Each of the kittens in a litter can have a different father.

One female cat and her offspring can produce 420,000 kittens in 7 years.

I just need some space.

A male cat can begin mating when he is between 7 and 10 months old and can continue to mate at 16 years old.

Neutering a male cat will stop him from spraying and fighting with other males, and will lengthen and improve the quality of his life.

How a cat holds its tail says a lot about its mood. When the tail is held high, the cat is happy. A twitching tail is a warning sign. When the tail is tucked close to the body, the cat is insecure.

All cats are born with blue eyes.

A cat's paws have sensitive touch receptors. Some researchers believe they can sense tiny vibrations.

The average cat consumes about 127,750 calories a year.

Cats need a high level of protein in their diets and can't digest a diet of grains, fruits, or vegetables.

Cats prefer to eat in a quiet spot at the same time every day.

Mmm. Just like Mama used to make.

Cats cannot produce fat on their own.

Cats do not like to have their whiskers
disturbed while eating.

As little as 16 ounces of chocolate can
kill a cat.

# MEOW LIKE AN EGYPTIAN

The Egyptians domesticated cats around 3,000 BC.

Ancient Egyptians believed that Bast was the mother of all cats.

Egyptians believed that cats were sacred animals.

Small Egyptian amulets representing cats date from as early as 2300 BC. The oldest picture of a cat was found in the tomb of Baket III. It dates from 1950 BC and shows a cat confronting a rat.

Well, Mrs. Frogworthy, that's the last you'll see of those pesky chair monsters.

In ancient Egypt, the penalty for killing a cat was death.

Ancient Egyptians thought that a cat washing its ears was a sign of good weather.

Cats of ancient Egypt were considered demigods and the property of divine Pharaoh, ranking them above humans.

It is rumored that cats were rescued from burning buildings before humans in ancient Egypt.

When the Persian army surrounded the Egyptian city of Memphis in the 6th century BC, they captured many cats and tortured them. The Egyptians surrendered because they didn't want any more cats to be injured.

The small African wildcat found an abundant food supply in the mice and rodents attacking the Egyptian grain supplies.

Ancient Egyptian family members shaved their eyebrows in mourning the death of the family cat.

Meet my best friend Goldie.
Hee hee hee.

I don't know. It said "drink me" and my head just started shrinking.

Dead cats were embalmed and buried in special coffins in their own cat-graveyards.

Homeless cats received a daily free meal after a 13th-century Egyptian sultan left his entire fortune to the needy cats of Cairo.

The Egyptian sun god Ra assumed the form of a tomcat each night for his battle with the serpent of darkness.

The ancient Egyptian word for cat was miou.

The goddess Bast was worshipped by the Egyptians in the form of a cat-headed woman with powers devoted to love and fertility.

Wonder what this key does. Oops!

In honor of Bast, the ancient city of Bubastis held an annual festival, which allowed excessive drinking and free sex. The festival lasted 3 days, and on the third night, a candle was lit inside the temple of Bast, spreading light throughout the city.

Large parts of the northern section of Bubastis, which means "realm of the cat," is a cat cemetery, joined by a cemetery of humans who wanted to be buried near the sacred animals. The cemetery once held more than 30,000 cat mummies.

Mice, rats, and bowls of milk were placed in cat tombs in Bubastis.

Now, Bast can be invoked to help with problems concerning domestic life, work situations, and success, as well as love and good health.

The Abyssinian cat, the favored descendant of Bast, is considered the "Child of the Gods."

Many cat statuettes decorated with jewelry have been found in tombs.

Please, please, please!

Egyptians are known for their
mummification of humans, but they also
mummified cats using 6 steps:
1. Remove organs;
2. Stuff body with sand or
packing material;
3. Place cat in a sitting position
4. Wrap body tightly;
5. Paint faces and designs on wrappings
with black ink;
6. Use no chemicals, only natural
dehydration.

It was illegal to export cats from Egypt,
but many were still taken to the
Mediterranean countries. Armies were
often sent to recapture the missing cats.

# CAT TAILS

In 1950, a 4-month-old kitten owned by a woman from Switzerland followed a group of climbers to the top of the Matterhorn in the Swiss Alps.

When one amazing feline turned 33, his owners celebrated by giving him a cake topped with tuna and asparagus.

A cat in Austin, Texas, eats a daily breakfast of bacon, eggs, coffee, and broccoli.

In September 1996, two rare "diamond-eyed" cats, Phet and Ploy, were married in matching pink outfits at a ceremony in Thailand.

Sshh! I'm trying to study.

The Pasadena, California, Humane Society has a cat named Maggie who functions as a dog tester. She determines if dogs are cat-friendly before they are given to families who already own cats.

A cat named Brownie became one of the richest pets in the world when his owner bequeathed him $415,000.

In Siam, the cat was so revered that it rode in a chariot at the head of a parade celebrating a new king.

In 1995 a metallic-colored domestic cat was discovered in a hayloft in northwest Denmark. It was determined that the cat had "a copper patina, apparently present since birth, from the tip of its fur to the hair follicles." However, it is unknown if the color was caused by a genetic mutation or exposure to copper.

On January 16, 2003, a cat named Shadow saved her owner, two young children, and a dog from carbon monoxide poisoning. Shadow meowed loudly until her owner awoke and got everyone out of the house.

Cuty Boy, a purebred Persian, answers "no" and "yes" to questions by shaking his head, kisses his owner's cheek, solves math problems, and knows 8 languages, including Gujarati, Persian, Malayalam, English, Arabic, and French.

What are you lookin' at?

At the Second Annual Cat Show at Madison Square Garden in 1896, one lucky owner of a brown tabby American Shorthair was offered $2,500 for his pet.

During a part of the Middle Ages the cat was persecuted by the Christian church and was associated with witchcraft and black magic. It became acceptable as a pet in the 18th century.

The Black Death in England was blamed on cats, leading thousands of people to kill theirs. However, those that did not were less affected by the plague because the cats kept their houses clear of the actual cause—rats.

Why does it keep coming back over here?

In Liege, Belgium, in 1879, several dozen cats were employed to carry bundles of letters to villages. They weren't disciplined in the trade, so the service didn't last long.

Hmm...tastes like chicken.

A couple in Istanbul, Turkey, owns 600 cats and one dog. The couple spends more than $2,000 a month on cat food and has 2 assistants to help tend to the cats.

A mother cat in Paarl, South Africa, once adopted 3 squirrels. She nursed them alongside her three kittens.

A one-year-old Persian named Sebastian sports gold crowns on his two bottom canines, which stick out from his lips like a bulldog. Each gold tooth cost about $900.

While tending her garden in July 2003, a woman was approached by an Eastern Cottonmouth snake. The woman's cat, Sosa, attacked the snake and was bitten on the paw, but saved her owner's life. Sosa survived the nearly fatal wound after spending 3 days at an animal hospital.

In 1888, an estimated 300,000 mummified cats were found at Beni Hassan, Egypt. They were sold at $18.43 per ton, and shipped to England to be ground up and used for fertilizer.

But, Mom!

Weavers in Baghdad were inspired by the colors and markings of cat coats.

The British Shorthair descended from the domestic cat of ancient Rome.

In 1930, Dr. Joseph Thompson of San Francisco introduced the first Burmese cat—Wong Mau—to the western world.

You forgot to add fabric softener.

While building the Grand Coulee Dam in the state of Washington, engineers had problems threading a cable through a pipeline. A cat was harnessed to the cable and crawled through the pipeline maze.

When a Missouri woman died in 1978, she left her entire estate to her cat with the stipulation that when her cat died, the remainder of the estate would be donated to humane societies.

During World War I, cats lived with soldiers in trenches, where they killed mice.

A Persian cat once saved his owner from a bear!

A company in Salt Lake City, Utah, mummifies cats for $4,500.

Several American Shorthair cats arrived on the *Mayflower* with the Pilgrims.

Parlez-vous français?

The Birman cat, a companion of the Kittah priests of Burma, was considered sacred.

The Chartreux cat was raised as a companion to the Carthusian monks.

Beau, a 4-year-old cat in Quebec, saved her owner (and herself) from burning to death in an apartment fire. Beau continuously threw herself against a bedroom door, waking her owner. The two hurried to a balcony, where they were rescued by the fire department.

Another cat, Étoile de Nuit, also saved her owner from a burning apartment. The cat woke up her owner, who in turn woke her neighbors. But when the woman went back for her cat, she had disappeared. The cat was finally found outside near the burning building.

Christening the new bed.

One amazing feline, Samantha, came to her owner, Tia, by chance and ended up saving her life during a fire. Tia suffered from many health problems, including poor eyesight, but she was able to train Samantha to help her find items she couldn't see. Now Samantha is a registered service animal.

Sshh! I'm trying to blend in with the floor.

A 5-year-old orange tabby named Hobbes saved his owner from yet another burning apartment building by yowling loudly.

A high school student named Jose was suffering from a potentially fatal seizure one night when his cat, Bart, ran to find the boy's mother and alert her. The boy was saved, and Bart was honored by the state of Illinois for her "ingenuity and persistence."

I'll get you, my pretty!

# LEGENDS OF
# THE PAW

Some people believe that a cat washing behind its ears indicates rain is coming.

Ancient mariners believed that a cat's behavior could foretell a change in the weather.

Tortoise-shell cats were often regarded by seafarers as lucky, and Japanese sailors in particular preferred to bring a tri-colored cat, or "Mi-Ki," aboard, believing that such a cat could give early warning of an approaching storm.

Some sailors, feeling especially credulous, would send the cat up the mast to "put the storm devils to flight."

What idiot would sing in the rain?

Polydactyl, or many-toed, cats were believed to be better at catching the pesky mice abundant aboard their ships.

Black cats, however, weren't usually invited on board as they were considered unlucky and thought to bring on bad weather.

Many seafarers believed if the ship's cat began to frolic, it signified the approach of a strong wind. When the cat jumped and played, they would say the cat had "a gale of wind in her tail."

The small ripples that are sometimes seen on the surface of an otherwise calm sea are known as "cat's paws" and are said to be caused by the ghosts of ancient ship's cats dancing ahead of the wind.

In ancient Thailand, the souls of spiritual people who died were believed to enter the body of a cat. Once the cat died, the soul went to heaven.

Seeing a cat with a paw uplifted brings good luck and fortune.

An ancient Japanese abbot kept several cats in the temple. After wishing his cats would bring him luck, a group of Samurais stopped at the temple to rest, allowing them to escape from an unexpected storm. In gratitude, the men became benefactors of the temple, restoring it to wealth and honor.

Gene Simmons is my idol.

A great noble and his entourage passed by the temple of Gotoku-ji, where they were welcomed by a cat with a raised paw. The noble entered the temple and, shortly thereafter, the spot where he had been standing was hit by lightning. Cats were later thought to be an incarnation of the Goddess of Mercy.

A starving cat turned up one day at the temple of Gotoku-ji begging for food. Despite their poverty, the monks fed the cat and restored it to health. Thus, the temple's prosperity was also restored. The monks believed that the cat had been a messenger from heaven and honored it as such.

Today, the Gotoku-ji temple in Tokyo is the home of the "Beckoning Cat," which is thought to bring good luck, protect domestic homes, and bring prosperity to businesses.

I know you're not trying to give me a bath—right?

The outside of the temple is liberally decorated with these "Maneki-Neko"— or sitting cats with one raised paw.

C'mon, I dare you!

Adjoining the temple is a cemetery where hundreds of cats are buried. There is a stone cat statue whose spirit is said to watch over the souls of the cats buried there. Owners whose cats have died come to the shrine to pray for the departed souls of their pets.

In Britain, fishermen's wives believed keeping a black cat in the home meant their husbands would always return from the sea.

In Russia, the Russian Blue cat is considered lucky.

The Hindu religion teaches that everyone is expected to take care of at least one cat during his or her lifetime.

I'm prettier! No, I'm prettier!
No, I am!

Ancient Chinese legend maintains that the cat is the offspring of a lioness and a monkey—the lioness bestowing her dignity and the monkey his curiosity and playfulness.

One ancient story tells of when Islamic prophet Mohammed's cat Muezza fell asleep on his sleeve. Rather than disturb the cat, the Prophet cut off his sleeve.

It is said that the "M" marking on the forehead of the tabby cat was created by Mohammed when he rested his hand on the brow of his favorite kitty.

In Norse mythology, the chariot of Freya, goddess of beauty, love, and fertility, is drawn by two large, longhaired cats. These two cats were connected with the powers of creativity, the Earth Mother, and fertility gods.

According to legend, the Bobtail is the Japanese cat of preference because it is less likely to "bewitch" you with a twitching tail.

In what was known as Bohemia, the cat was regarded as a symbol of fertility.

There are still people who regard cats as bad luck—some believe that the cat is a reincarnation of the devil.

Where's my halo?

Once many years ago several kittens were thrown into a river to drown. While the mother cat wept in despair, the surrounding willow trees felt compassion and held out their branches to the struggling kittens, who clung to them and were saved. Ever since, willow trees develop gray buds in springtime that feel as soft and silky as kitten tails.

A white cat sitting on your doorstep before your wedding is a sign of lasting happiness.

# CRAZY CAT
# LAWS

In the 9th century, King Henry I of Saxony decreed that the fine for killing a cat was 60 bushels of corn.

In Sterling, Colorado, it is unlawful for a cat to run loose without a taillight.

In French Lick Springs, Indiana, a law was passed requiring all black cats to wear bells on Friday the 13th.

In Zion, Illinois, it's illegal to give lighted cigars to cats.

It is illegal for a cat to fight a dog in Barbar, North Carolina.

In Ventura County, California, cats and dogs cannot have sex without a permit.

Cats may not yowl after 9 p.m. in Columbus, Georgia.

While Ronald Reagan was governor of California, he signed a bill that outlawed kicking cats.

Make mine overeasy with a side of bacon.

The 13th-century English "Rule of Nuns" stated the holy women could keep no animal but the cat.

Wow, just think what kind of damage I could do at the dollar store!

In 1818, a decree was issued at Ypres in Flanders, Belgium, forbidding the throwing of felines from high towers in commemoration of a Christmas Spectacle.

Madison, Wisconsin, will not allow joint custody of a family pet when a couple divorces—the animal is legally awarded to whomever happens to have possession of it at the time of the initial separation.

In Duluth, Minnesota, cats may not sleep in a bakery.

In Topeka, Kansas, you may not own more than 5 cats at a time.

In Shorewood, Wisconsin, a family cannot own more than 2 cats at a time.

You may not keep a pet cat and a pet bird on the same premises in Reed City, Michigan.

Cats living in Cresskill, New Jersey, must wear three bells to warn birds of their whereabouts.

In Lorinc, Hungary, cats can only be taken on to the street on leashes.

Whew! Being cute is exhausting.

In Kentucky, dogs are not allowed to attack or bother cats, though they can legally fight with each other.

Cats in International Falls, Minnesota, are not allowed to chase dogs up telephone poles.

Saudi Arabia's religious police banned the sale of pet cats and dogs.

# OUTRAGEOUS
# CAT OWNERS

Half of cat owners never take their pets to a veterinarian.

Ernest Hemingway was once given a 6-toed polydactyl cat by a friendly sea captain in his hometown of Key West, Florida. Today, around 60 cats still make their home at the Hemingway Home & Museum, many of which are descendants of this famous cat.

Stroking a cat can lower a person's blood pressure.

George Burns called his cat "Willie," supposedly because, "when you told the cat what to do, it was always a question of will he or won't he."

Chicks dig a man with a bike.

Americans spend more than $5.4 billion on their pets each year.

Sir Winston Churchill's cat Jock attended many wartime Cabinet meetings, and meals at the Churchill household could not begin until the tabby was at the table. Jock slept with his master and was with Churchill when he died.

Churchill had another cat, Nelson, named for a famous British admiral.

More money is spent on cat food each year than on baby food.

Most American pet owners obtain their cats by adopting strays.

Nostradamus had a cat named Grimalkin, which can be defined as "a cat, especially an old female cat" or "an old woman considered to be ill-tempered."

More than 40 percent of pet owners admit to talking to their pets over the phone.

Can you hear me now?

A cat pushing its face against your head
is a sign of acceptance and affection.

Abraham Lincoln came to office
accompanied by Tabby, a cat belonging to
his son. Tabby was the first of several
White House cats.

Sir Isaac Newton preferred not to be
interrupted during his research, but he
wanted to grant his cats the liberty to
wander in and out even when the doors
were closed. Thus, he invented the
cat door.

Twenty-five percent of pet owners say they blow-dry their pet's hair after a bath.

Edward Lear had his home in England replicated in San Remo, Italy, so that when he moved, his tabby Foss would not be distressed by the change in scenery.

Lear's drawings of his striped tabby are well known, especially those that accompany his rhyme, "The Owl and the Pussycat."

Almost half of all cat owners admit to carrying a picture of their pet in their wallet.

Twenty-one percent of cat owners admit to occasionally dressing up their pets.

Sir Walter Scott loved cats, and even had John Watson Gordon paint a portrait of him working at his desk with his tabby, Hinx, lying close by.

More than half of cat owners give their cats a human name.

Fifty-eight percent of pets are included in family and holiday portraits.

What did I do to deserve this?

Seventy-nine percent of cat owners give their pets presents for birthdays and holidays.

What did you get me—another stupid toy mouse?

Alexandre Dumas's cat, Mysouff II, was discovered with a belly full of Dumas's entire exotic bird collection. Dumas held a mock trial to determine the cat's fate and sentenced it to 5 years imprisonment in a cage with Dumas's monkeys. Shortly thereafter, Dumas had to sell the monkeys, freeing the cat.

Harriet Beecher Stowe had a large Maltese cat called Calvin (the same name as her husband), who often sat on her shoulder as she wrote.

Florence Nightingale owned more than 60 cats during her lifetime.

Edgar Allan Poe used cats as sinister symbols in several of his stories, although he owned and loved cats. His tortoise-shell cat Catarina was the inspiration for his story "The Black Cat."

In winter 1846, Catarina would curl up on the bed with Poe's wife, who was dying of tuberculosis, and provide her warmth.

Seventy percent of owners sign their pet's name on greeting cards.

Interesting. Very interesting.

People who own cats experience less stress, have fewer heart attacks, and live longer.

What's a cat have to do to get a water bowl around here?

Dr. Schweitzer rescued a lost kitten in a building under construction and named her Sizi. She sat on his desk as he wrote, often falling asleep on his left arm. In order to not disturb her, Dr. Schweitzer, who was left-handed, would write prescriptions with his right hand.

Another cat, Piccolo, slept on papers stacked on Schweitzer's desk. If someone needed the papers, they were required to wait until the cat awoke.

Mark Twain kept 11 cats at his farm in Connecticut. He wrote, "I simply can't resist a cat, particularly a purring one. They are the cleanest, cunningest, and most intelligent things I know, outside of the girl you love, of course."

Domenico Scarlatti's cat, Pulcinella, was fond of prancing about on the harpsichord, which led to *Fugue in G Minor*, better known as *The Cat's Fugue*. Of course, Scarlatti may have helped a little, but the first few bars are convincingly the work of a cat.

Over half of pet owners report that their pets get more exercise than they do.

Go away. My soap's on.

When Caroline Kennedy's cat Tom Kitten died, it was given an obituary in a Washington newspaper.

If I can only stay awake, I'll ace that exam.

Among Amy Carter's several cats was the oddly named "Misty Malarky Ying Yang" who lived with her in the White House.

The first Siamese cat brought to the United States was a gift to President Rutherford B. Hayes.

Other presidents who owned cats: William McKinley, Ronald Reagan, Teddy Roosevelt, Woodrow Wilson, and Bill Clinton.

T.S. Eliot was a cat lover who wrote an entire book of poems about cats. His *Old Possum's Book of Practical Cats* was set to music by Andrew Lloyd Weber and became the long-running musical, *Cats*.

Charles Dickens' cat, Willamena, once produced a litter of kittens in his study. Dickens was determined not to keep the kittens, but he fell in love with one female who became known as "Master's Cat." This cunning cat knew how to get her master's attention—she simply snuffed out his reading candle.

Robert E. Lee had several furry friends that he referred to often in letters to his family: "I am very solitary and my only company is my dog and cats." He chose cats to share his tent at Camp Cooper, partly for catching mice and partly for company.

I see a handsome stranger in your future...

When he wasn't writing timeless classics like *Les Misérables*, Victor Hugo wrote fondly of his cats in his diary.

Now about that belly rub...

Charles Lindbergh's cat Pasty often accompanied him on his flights, although he didn't take her on the flight that made him famous. A Spanish stamp commemorating his record-breaking flight from New York to Paris showed Patsy watching as his plane took off.

Frédéric Chopin's cat also walked across his keyboard, inspiring the melody, *The Cat Waltz*.

But not everyone loves cats. Genghis Kahn was a famous cat-hater as were Alexander the Great, Julius Caesar, and Dwight D. Eisenhower.

The same streak of ailurophobia influenced Napoleon Bonaparte, Benito Mussolini, and Adolph Hitler.

Henry III, despite his bold and fearless stature, would faint on the spot if a cat happened to wander into his presence.

# FAMOUS
# FELINES

The first full-length feature film with a feline star was *Gay Purr-ee*, made in the 1960s. Judy Garland was the voice of Mewsette, the star.

The first animated cat was Krazy Kat, a cartoon strip drawn by George Herriman that made the transition from paper to film in 1916.

Created by Jim Davis in 1978, the lasagna-loving Garfield was the star of a comic strip that appeared in 1,000 newspapers around the world within 4 years.

Although Morris went on to become America's most famous commercial cat, he came from humble beginnings—he was rescued from a Chicago animal shelter by Bob Martwick, a professional animal trainer.

Got milk?

Morris became spokes-cat for Purina's 9 Lives cat food in 1969, and eventually became honorary director of Star-Kist Foods, with veto power over any flavor he didn't like.

President Nixon invited Morris to co-sign, or paw-print, the National Animal Protection Bill.

Tom and his love-hate pal Jerry, have chased each other to the moon and back, and some 50 years after their debut, are still at it.

Created by Australian Pat Sullivan, Felix was the star of the first "talkie" cartoon, a year before Mickey Mouse began to talk. Felix was also the subject of the very first television test broadcasts in 1928.

Dr. Seuss's magical book *The Cat in the Hat* was the end-result of an assignment to write a children's primer using 220 new-reader vocabulary words. While schools were hesitant to adopt it as an official primer, flocks of children and parents bought copies.

The Picture Animal Top Star of the Year, or PATSY, Award was developed in Hollywood by the American Humane Association in 1939, with the desire to honor animal performers. The award has 4 categories: canine, equine, wild, and special. Cats fall into the "special" category.

Bah humbug!

A hard-working orange and black tabby, Orangey, appeared in the movies *Rhubarb, Gigot,* and *Breakfast at Tiffany's,* as well as the television series, *Our Miss Brooks.* She was a PATSY Award recipient in 1952 and 1962.

Please don't eat me! I'll leave your shoelaces alone, I promise!

Peggy Lee was the voice of Am and Si, the devious Siamese cats of Disney's *Lady and the Tramp*.

The cartoon character Heathcliff was named after the character from *Wuthering Heights*.

Pepper was a gray alley cat who became a movie star simply by wandering onto a set. She went on to star in many silent films alongside Charles Murray, Fanny Kelly, and Chester Conklin.

Sneaky Pie Brown helps her owner, writer Rita Mae Brown, work out plot lines for mystery novels.

Panther, a gold tabby, played the newspaper-bearing cat on *Early Edition*.

SGC Belfry Ted Nude-Gent, a Sphynx, played Dr. Evil's cat Mr. Bigglesworth in the Austin Powers movies.

# CAT MYTHS
# UNVEILED

Myth: Cats always land on their feet.

Fact: While cats instinctively fall feet first and may survive falls from high places, they don't always land on their feet and aren't immune to broken bones in the process.

Myth: Cats should drink milk everyday.

Fact: Most cats like milk, but do not need it on a daily basis if properly nourished. In fact, they may get diarrhea if they drink too much milk.

Myth: Cats can't get rabies.

Fact: Actually, most warm-blooded mammals, including cats, bats, skunks, and ferrets, can carry rabies. Cats need regular vaccinations, just like dogs.

I've fallen and I can't get up.

Myth: Cats that are spayed or neutered automatically gain weight.

Fact: They gain weight from eating too much, not exercising enough, or both. In many cases, spaying or neutering is done at an older age when the animal is no longer growing and its metabolism has slowed. So, if the cat continues to eat the same amount, it may gain weight.

Myth: Tapeworms come from bad food.

Fact: Pets actually become infected with tapeworms from swallowing fleas, which carry the parasite. Cats can also get tapeworms from eating infected mice or other exposed animals.

Myth: Animals heal themselves by licking their wounds.

Fact: Licking can actually slow the healing process and irritate the wound.

Myth: Pregnant women shouldn't own cats.

Fact: Although some cats can be infected with a disease called toxoplasmosis, which occasionally can be spread to humans through litter boxes and cause serious problems in unborn babies, these problems can be controlled if the expectant mother avoids contact with the litter box (and fecal matter) during her pregnancy.

Myth: A cat's sense of balance is in its whiskers.

Fact: They use their whiskers to "feel" their way around, but not to maintain their balance.

Are you my mother?

Myth: Putting garlic on a pet's food will
get rid of worms.

Fact: While it may make the animal's
food taste better, it has no effect on
worms.

OK, now I want to be on top.

# EXTRA, EXTRA, BREED ALL ABOUT IT!

The Maine Coon cat is the only breed of domestic feline indigenous to America.

Bombay cats can have eye color ranging from gold to deep copper, the latter being considered superior.

The Siberian is the national breed of Russia and is extremely rare in the United States.

The woolly fur of the Chartreux contributed to its name, which is a type of Spanish wool.

Many Chartreux are completely mute; they purr, but cannot meow.

There are about 100 different breeds of domestic cats.

Housecats are descendants of the African wildcat—a small brown tabby that is now an endangered species.

Yes, I do like my tail.

The American Curl cat has unique curled ears that are the result of a spontaneous mutation and give the breed a happy and alert look.

Ever heard of squatter's rights?

Savannahs can be recognized by the "tear drop" markings around their eyes.

Six-toed kittens are so common in Boston that experts consider it an established mutation.

The fishing cat, an excellent swimmer found in India and Pakistan, finds most of its prey in the water—frogs, reptiles, and, of course, fish.

Not always completely hairless, the Sphynx can have hair on its nose, tail, and toes. The texture of its skin has been compared to suede.

The Siberian, Maine Coon, and Norwegian Forest cats have slightly oily, water-repellent top coats and thick, insulating undercoats to help them survive in cold climates.

In the Siamese cat, a lower temperature causes more dark coloration in the growing hairs.

Some cats are anurous (without tails) because of a genetic mutation.

What am I really? Mom? Mom?

The Birman cat's white feet, known as gloves and laces, are ideally symmetrical.

The miacis, which had a long body and tail and short legs, was the earliest ancestor of the cat.

Bet you wish you could do this!

Japanese Bobtails like to carry things in their mouths, play fetch, and ride on their owners' shoulders.

Burmese have dog-like tendencies. They love to shadow their owners and play fetch.

Abyssinians look like cats in the paintings and sculptures of ancient Egypt.

The Devon Rex has been described as "a cross between a cat, a monkey, and Dennis the Menace."

Korats are very protective of their owners. Although they mix well with other cats, they like to have their owners' full attention.

The Manx cat, which originated on the Isle of Man (off the coast of England), is a mutation of the island's domestic cats.

The Egyptian Mau is the only natural spotted breed of domestic cat.

How did I end up here?

The British Shorthair is often used in Hollywood films and television commercials.

Persians are the most popular breed in America.

One mouse... two mice... three mice...

The only spotted domestic breed selectively bred to emulate the cats of the wild, the Ocicat was interbred from the Abyssinian, Siamese, and American Shorthair.

The Havana Brown easily learns its name and the word "No." It makes a great traveling companions in a car or airplane.

Female RagaMuffins weigh an average of 10 to 15 pounds, while males weigh about 15 to 20 pounds.

Woo-hoo! I lost 4 ounces!

The Cornish Rex first appeared in a litter of barn cats in Cornwall, England.

Often selected as Best in Show, American Shorthairs are big winners at cat shows.

The sand cat, found mainly in Africa, burrows into the sand to protect itself from the heat of the sun during the day.

The Russian Blue, Queen Victoria's favorite pet, is a descendant of the royal cat of the Russian czars.

The Selkirk Rex's owners often hear their cats referred to as "having a bad hair day."

Ragdolls shed very little, have very few hairballs, and should be groomed with a steel comb.

# CAT NIP

In Asian Buddhist temples, cats are kept as mousers.

There are more than 75 million cats in the United States. There are about 500 million pet cats in the world.

Cats use the earth's magnetic fields to navigate their way home.

Ailurophobia is the fear of cats.

All domestic cats are members of the
same species—*Felis catus*.

I hope my face doesn't freeze like this.

Cats live longer than most dogs.

In cat years, middle age begins at 7, and by 10, a cat is considered old.

Cats have a vocal range of as many as 60 notes.

Under normal circumstances, a cat can run up to 25 mph, but a frightened cat can reach 30 mph.

Most cats spend 70 percent of the day sleeping and 15 percent grooming.

Non-pedigree cats tend to live longer than pedigree cats.

The 2 most popular cat names in the U.S. are Tiger and Samantha.

Cats outnumber dogs by millions as house pets.

This doesn't look like any mouse
I've ever seen.

The cat is the only domestic animal not mentioned in the Bible.

Dude, can we just go already?

Cats lose almost as much fluid in saliva while grooming themselves as they do through urination.

Extremely high-pitched musical notes cause agitation in many cats.

Cat urine glows in UV light.

A cat can jump 5 times its height.

It was discovered in the 1930s that the note E of the fourth octave made young cats defecate and adult cats sexually excited.

Cats have a greater chance surviving a 20-story fall than a 7-story fall because it takes them about 8 floors to realize what is happening, relax, and correct themselves.

The average lifespan for the domestic cat is between 9 and 15 years.

Roaring is in the eye of the beholder.

Although litter sizes vary, 4 to 5 is the
average.

The cat's IQ is surpassed only by that of monkeys and chimps.

Cats respond better to names that end in an "ee" sound.

I'm sorry; I just couldn't breathe in there.

Cats have been domesticated for half as long as dogs have been.

Domestic cats are the only species able to hold their tail vertical while walking.

Cats purr at about 26 cycles per second.

Cats love having their forehead and faces stroked.

A cat will tremble, shiver, or even purr when it is in extreme pain.

One in 3 pounces results in a catch.

The average lifespan of an outdoor cat is about 3 years.

Lean-bodied cats are more likely to be outgoing, protective, and vocal than those with a stocky build.

Cat bites are more likely to become infected than dog bites.

Cat families play best in even numbers.

Don't think I can't see you.

# Kitty litter was invented in 1947 by Edward Lowe.

Yes, this is my house. Why?

Meowing is a sound reserved for humans.

A cat cannot see directly under its nose.

Cats can be right-pawed or left-pawed.

Cats bury their feces to cover their trails from predators.

The first signs of predatory behavior occur when kittens are around 4 weeks old.

Cats lick themselves to smooth their fur and get rid of the "human" smell.

The cat has a high level of intelligence, can remember problem solving strategies, and uses insight to "think" its way out of situations. Curiosity stems from this intelligence.

Chemicals can be absorbed through a cat's paws.

I'm working on my audition for the kitty version of <u>Wicked</u>.

Catnip, which is not addictive, excites cats because it contains a chemical that resembles an excretion of the dominant female's urine.

Only 80 percent of cats respond to catnip; the other 20 percent are missing the gene that causes them to react.

The effects of catnip last about 6 minutes. Males have stronger reactions than females.

Cats younger than 6 months old show no interest in catnip.

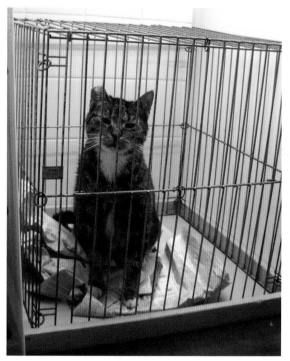

You're the cutest jailbird I ever did see.

Cats wag their tails when they are in a stage of conflict.

Finders keepers!

In the 17th and 18th centuries, catnip tea was believed to have medicinal powers and was often prescribed by doctors to cure various ailments.

Cats can donate blood to other cats.

The phrase "raining cats and dogs" originated in 17th-century England. During heavy downpours of rain, many of these animals drowned and their bodies would be seen floating in the streets, making it appear to have literally rained cats and dogs.

Neutered males live an average of 3 years longer than non-neutered males and are more resistant to infection.

A cat's memory can last as long as 16 hours.

Cats age 10 years in the first 6 months of their lives.

Some types of raw fish can cause a vitamin deficiency in cats.

Cats were brought to America by colonists as pets and to protect their granaries.

Human painkillers, such as acetaminophen, are toxic to cats.

Are we moving?

What, are you afraid or something?

Tuna fish makes a cat's heart muscle rubbery.

Cats lap liquid from the underside of their tongue rather than from the top.

Cat scratch fever is caused by bacteria and can be spread through many animals, not just cats.

Why do you think they call it a cat nap,
dummy?

U.S. animal shelters are forced to put
down 30,000 cats and dogs everyday.

Each year 1 out of 170 people in the
U.S. is bitten by a cat.